IMAGES
of America

AROUND
DEAL LAKE

ALLENHURST, DEAL,
INTERLAKEN, AND
LOCH ARBOUR

Many postcards were produced depicting Deal Lake, beginning in the late 1890s, when the communities surrounding it began to develop. Described in an early deed between the Lenape Indians and Gavin Drummond as "Great Pond," Deal Lake was also referred to on early maps as White's Pond, Corlies Pond, and Boyleston's Pond, in accordance with surrounding land ownership.

IMAGES
of America

AROUND
DEAL LAKE

ALLENHURST, DEAL,
INTERLAKEN, AND
LOCH ARBOUR

Marie A. Sylvester

ARCADIA

First published 1998
Copyright © Marie A. Sylvester, 1998

ISBN 0-7524-0969-7

Published by Arcadia Publishing,
an imprint of the Chalford Publishing Corporation,
One Washington Center, Dover, New Hampshire 03820.
Printed in Great Britain

Library of Congress Cataloging-in-Publication Data applied for

*This book is dedicated to all those
who have provided me with their sincere interest and encouragement,
most specifically among them, my husband, Michael A. Sylvester.*

Cover Photograph: The guests of William P. and Suzanne Ahnelt gathered in the sunken gardens of their estate in Deal (see p. 76). (Paul Imgrund and Ann Steen.)

Contents

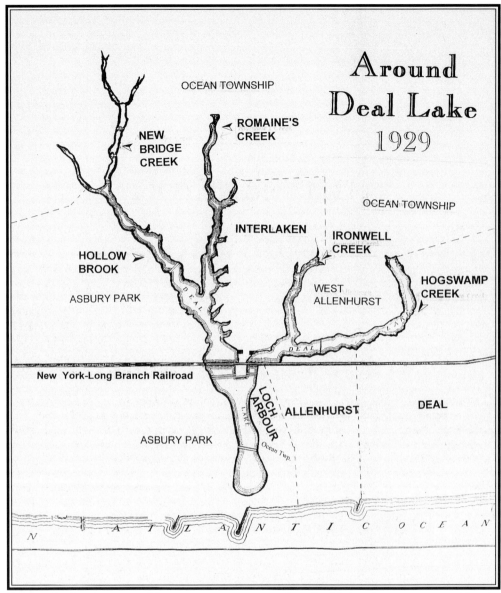

Around
Deal Lake
1929

OCEAN TOWNSHIP

ROMAINE'S
CREEK

NEW
BRIDGE
CREEK

OCEAN TOWNSHIP

INTERLAKEN

IRONWELL
CREEK

HOLLOW
BROOK

HOGSWAMP
CREEK

ASBURY PARK

WEST
ALLENHURST

DEAL

New York-Long Branch Railroad

LOCH ARBOUR

ALLENHURST

DEAL

ASBURY PARK

Ocean Twp.

ATLANTIC OCEAN

N

Prior to the development of the communities surrounding Deal Lake, the area was considered a desirable location, attracting the first summer visitors long before any beach pavilions or cabanas were built. By way of either the Minisink Trail or Burlington Path, the Lenape Indians migrated to this area to take advantage of the abundant wild fruit and game, clear running springs, lakes and oceans filled with fish, and cooler temperatures.

Introduction

The four communities reflected in this volume can be thought of as siblings borne of the parent community of Ocean Township, which was carved out of the vast land mass known as Shrewsbury Township in 1849. The metes and bounds description at that time utilized the borders of land owners such as Whyte, Castley, Spinning, Skulthorp, and Tilton. Still a very large tract of land, the Township of Ocean at that time included what is today Eatontown, Neptune Township, Neptune City, Avon, Bradley Beach, Ocean Grove, Asbury Park, Allenhurst, Deal, Long Branch, West Long Branch, Interlaken, Loch Arbour, Monmouth Beach, Oceanport, and Sea Bright. Within the large township, many smaller communities had begun to take shape, and in the spirit of independence their inhabitants sought complete control over the thriving communities they had worked to build.

Eatontown started the parade of secession in 1873, and would later wish West Long Branch and Oceanport good luck as they in turn separated from Eatontown in 1908 and 1920 respectively. Neptune Township followed suit in 1879, taking with it land that would eventually become Asbury Park, Bradley Beach, Avon, and Neptune City. Sea Bright was established in 1889, Long Branch in 1904, and Monmouth Beach in 1906.

However, the first to leave the nest from our area of focus was Allenhurst, in 1897. Up until 1894 the majority of the land that now makes up Allenhurst was owned by three Allen brothers, who farmed the 120-acre tract as early as 1846. Another large tract of land, some 20 acres lying to the east of the Allen holdings, was owned by Gilbert M. Spier, an attorney from New York City. Both of these large parcels were included in an area north of Deal Lake referred to as Deal Beach. The Allens had the most presence due to the establishment of a boarding house early on in their old farmhouse. The Allen House hosted visitors who wished to enjoy the thrill of ocean bathing at the quiet less-developed beaches in the area. The establishment of a residential community began in 1895 when Edwin P. Benjamin and James M. Ralston of the Coast Land Company purchased the Allen Farm and began plans for the creation of roads and building lots. As interest grew the Spier property along with other scattered parcels were acquired. The physical transformation of farmland to an exquisite residential community was accomplished at such a quick pace that those who had visited in the summer of 1895 returned the following season just to see the much publicized changes. On April 26, 1897, the Borough of Allenhurst was officially recognized and a council form of government was established with E.P. Benjamin in place as the borough's first mayor.

Following soon after, in 1898, the borough of Deal emerged as an independent community. Early deeds for the tract of land that was to become the borough of Deal include two settlers from Deal, England. Thomas Potter, arriving soon after the Monmouth Land Patent was begun in 1665, lived in a cave along a branch of the "Great Pond" called Hogswamp Creek. In 1675 Potter sold land to Thomas Whyte, who constructed a two-story homestead in the area of what is presently Norwood and Deal Esplanade. The first significant attempt at development occurred in 1893 when the Deal Beach Land Company purchased the Whyte property from the heirs of Thomas Whyte. By early 1894, Theodore S. Darling of Asbury Park acquired the southern third of the tract presently known as Deal. With the construction of the first railroad station and selected cottages, this area carried the name Darlington for the brief period of 1894 until 1897. In 1897, the Deal Beach Land Company sold the property to the Atlantic Coast Realty Company, an organization comprised of many wealthy and prominent business men, having both the financial means and social status to create an elite seashore community. The land purchase included the entire settlement of Deal Beach and the majority of the property extending north to Elberon. It attracted the attention of real estate enthusiasts as it was considered to be the largest commercial land transaction along the Jersey Coast. In March of 1898, the community of Deal was organized and its reputation as a resort for the privileged became well publicized in the local and New York newspapers.

The first mayor and council of Interlaken took their seats on June 26, 1922. Originally part of the tract of land purchased from the Lenape Indians by Gavin Drummond in 1687, in 1885 it captured the hearts of a prominent Boston physician Dr. Francis Weld and his wife, Fannie. They purchased the 364-acre tract in 1888 and established the Interlaken Farm, named after a similar peninsular community in Interlaken, Switzerland, where they had recently traveled. In 1890, Dr. Weld formed the Interlaken Land Company and plans to convert his farm into an exclusive residential cottage community soon took shape. Initial attempts failed due to the strict building requirements and the property was taken over by the International Trust Company of Boston by default. The development management firm of the Stormfeltz-Loveley-Neville Company was hired by the bank to bring the project to completion. Under new management the community continued to grow and soon attracted many artists, writers, and musicians who found the quiet location around Deal Lake an inspiring location to practice their arts. When Interlaken seceded from Ocean Township pessimists predicted that the baby borough would not be able to support itself. The borough of Interlaken remains today a strictly residential community, just as the original developers had intended.

In 1957, the village of Loch Arbour, the smallest of the four communities reflected in this volume, sought independence from Ocean Township due to conflicting views of development and construction. Ironically, the area of land that became known as Loch Arbour appears to have been established and laid out as a community prior to Allenhurst, Deal, or Interlaken, but it was the last to break away from Ocean Township. Early land transaction records indicate that Jacob Corlies acquired this tract from Abner Allen in 1820. In 1865, Mary and Edward Boyle were the owners of 65 acres located on the northern shore of Deal Lake, or Great Pond as it was called then. Mr. Boyle was a civil engineer, employed by the City of New York. He lived in a house that was relocated to what was then the west side of Deal Turnpike (Norwood Avenue) near the bridge crossing Deal Lake toward present-day Asbury Park. In 1881, Mr. and Mrs. Boyle died while on holiday in Europe, leaving no heirs. The property remained in limbo until it was acquired by Dr. Samuel Johnson for $11,000. Johnson teamed up with entrepreneur R. Tenbroeck Stout and together they began plans for the development of the tract now known as Loch Arbour in 1882.

The proximity of the ocean beaches drew many visitors to seashore localities; however, since small watercraft on the ocean were not yet common place, it was the Deal Lake that provided these shore communities with added attraction. Many journeyed here as guests of the grand hotels or stayed contentedly in adequate rooming houses. Others, possessing the wealth to do so, built stately homes on wide avenues, with a view of the breakers. Whether intentional or not, they created the foundation for these unique communities, which are still admired today.

Author's Note: Combining the four towns of Allenhurst, Deal, Interlaken, and Loch Arbour proved to be a laborious task in assuring an equal representation of each municipality. If any inequities exist it is most likely due to the lack of available materials on the subject, and not a disregard for its importance.

One

The Borough of Allenhurst

The original Allen House was both a guest house and residence of Judah Allen, owner of the tract which comprises the larger portion of present-day Allenhurst. Located on what was Stone Road (now Norwood Avenue) between Corlies and Allen Avenues, the early inn can be credited with attracting many prominent visitors to this area of the coast. The large farmhouse was sold along with the entire Allen Farm to the Coast Land Improvement Company in 1895.

Following the purchase of the Allen Farm in 1895, Edwin P. Benjamin and James M. Ralston organized the Coast Land Improvement Company. The enterprisers made constructing homes inexpensive by purchasing huge quantities of building materials. Even though they charged for labor and materials only, substantial profits were made on the sale of lots alone. (Leon S. Avakian, Inc.)

10

Edwin P. Benjamin kept shop as a real estate agent in Allenhurst prior to embarking on his development venture with James M. Ralston. Benjamin was elected the first mayor of Allenhurst and served in that capacity until 1900, when he became a councilman. (Allenhurst Centennial Committee.)

This caricature of James M. Ralston was part of a series of similar illustrations titled "Just for Fun" done in 1908 depicting prominent businessmen in the Asbury Park vicinity. Ralston, who was the president of Merchants National Bank in Asbury Park, also served as mayor of Allenhurst from 1902 through 1912. He was again named as mayor in 1916 following the transition of government from council form to committee. (Frederick A. Smith Jr.)

11

The enlarged Allenhurst Inn served as the starting point for the annual carriage parade which took place every August 10 to commemorate the acquisition of the property by the Coast Land Improvement Company. Following the parade a formal ball was held on the front lawn. In this image, taken in 1898, a large portion of Stone Road (Norwood Avenue) has been overtaken by handsome cabs organizing for the parade.

Occupying Allenhurst Inn cottage number two, Uzal H. McCarter prepares to set off for the annual carriage parade. McCarter served as the president of Fidelity Trust Company in Newark, New Jersey, and was one of many early summer visitors to Allenhurst from northern New Jersey.

The 12 inn cottages were constructed as part of the expansion of the Allenhurst Inn in 1899 to ease the large demand for accommodations during the summer months. Cottage number one, shown here, was located on Corlies Avenue, directly behind the main structure.

Modifications were made to the inn in 1899 by the Coast Land Improvement Company, including a proper full-length porch and upstairs verandah providing the appearance of a fine hotel. It could now accommodate 350 guests in the main house, and offered the convenience of gas, electricity, and even an elevator. An early morning fire destroyed the building in 1901. (Monmouth County Historical Association.)

A new hotel was built on the site of the Allenhurst Inn in 1903 under the management of Arthur B. Hammond. This postcard, stamped August 12, 1903, shows the Allenhurst Club shortly after its construction. It featured custom-designed bricks kilned at the Fisher brickyards, which was owned by an Allenhurst resident. On December 20, 1929, the building, like its predecessor, was destroyed by fire.

The structure above represents the final chapter in the Allenhurst Inn trilogy. This one-story structure occupied the site following the fire of the Allenhurst Club in 1929. During World War II the inn was used along with other structures in the borough to house the U.S. Army Signal Corps. In 1951, the building's ownership passed to the Borough and it was eventually sold at a public auction in 1956. (Allenhurst Centennial Committee.)

The Hotel Curlew and cottages was located on Allen Avenue opposite the pool and casino. Purchased by Edourd J. Solomons in 1916 from Jean Venetor, the hotel underwent significant improvements in order to compete with the Allenhurst Inn. The hotel was destroyed by a fire which originated in the basement in July 1931. (Robert Speck Collection.)

The "Writing Room" in the Hotel Curlew was located on the first floor facing Allen Avenue. (Roberta Chase.)

In 1858, Gilbert M. Spier, a prominent attorney from Manhattan, purchased 30 acres from Abner Allen. He constructed this Federal-style home amidst the thick grove of pines and white cedars set back from what is presently Norwood Avenue. Spier named his homestead "Belltrees," after his ancestral home in Scotland. (Long Branch Free Public Library.)

In 1897, the Coast Land Improvement Company acquired the Spier property and the already-established roads were continued through the property. Substantial changes were made to the Spier homestead, which could now be clearly identified as located at the southwest corner of Cedar and Ocean Avenues. Edwin P. Benjamin, president of the Coast Land Improvement Company, occupied the house for several years. This photograph of the Benjamin family seated on the back lawn of the house was taken around 1897.

This is how the Spier home appeared in 1906 when it was the residence of Edwin W. Scott. The home was also rented to Hubert T. Parsons, president of the F.W. Woolworth Company, prior to his purchase of the Shadow Lawn estate in West Long Branch. (Lee Elmer.)

The carriage house was also remodeled in the Neo-Classic Colonial-Revival style. During the mid-1920s through 1940, the mansion was used as a hotel known as "The Cedars." Following a fire in late 1940, the Borough of Allenhurst acquired the property through foreclosure and both structures were razed in 1943. (Lee Elmer.)

The Dunes Hotel was the only establishment of its kind located directly overlooking the bluff. The 85-room hotel was built in 1894 on property that is today between Corlies and Spier Avenue. The hotel prospered for 18 years until a fire on July 8, 1912, swept through the building, leaving many afternoon bathers on the beach without proper attire for dinner. Demolition of the building allowed for the continuation of Ocean Place in 1913.

This shot, taken in 1920, depicts the borough's early trash collection buggy on Corlies Avenue looking west. The Dunes Hotel (top of this page) was located just to the east of this view. (Allenhurst Centennial Committee.)

Following the sale of their family's land to the Coast Land Improvement Company in 1895, two Allen brothers and one of their sisters constructed homes on Corlies Avenue. This is the home and carriage house of Ezekiel C. Allen. It still stands today at 216 Corlies Avenue.

It is believed that the young boys posing in this photograph are the children of Ezekiel Allen. The Allen home (above) is visible in the background and Corlies Avenue appears to be barely established. This is one of a series of card mounted photographs taken by Alfred S. Campbell in 1896. (Monmouth County Historical Association.)

The summer home of Alfred S. Campbell was located on Corlies and Lake Avenues. Campbell was the vice president of Citizens National Bank and was among the original group of prominent business men to construct homes in Allenhurst. He was also a very progressed photographer, capturing many vintage scenes of early Allenhurst. It is believed the house was either moved or razed in conjunction with road realignment in the 1920s.

The residence of Frank E. Wright took up several lots on the eastern section of Corlies Avenue near the railroad station. Mr. Wright, like many of Allenhurst's residents during this time, was a seasonal visitor to the borough, keeping a home in Philadelphia. He was the president of Syndicate Publishing Company, Philadelphia.

This landmark home at the corner of Allen Avenue and Lake Avenue (Ocean Avenue) was built in 1896. President McKinley's brother, who either rented or visited the residence, utilized the tower to watch the carriage parades from the Allenhurst Inn. The home remains today virtually unchanged at 24 Allen Avenue.

This completely brick home was located at the southeast corner of Norwood Avenue and Allen Avenue. The home was built using bricks from Fisher's brickyards as an advertisement for the company. In 1943, it housed military personnel from the U.S. Army Signal Corps. In 1954, when efforts to sell the home proved futile, the owners opted to have the house demolished in order to subdivide the land. (United States Army Communications Electronics Museum.)

The Mediterranean-style home at 1 Spier Avenue was the home of Byron and Julie Creamer from 1924 to 1948. Mr. Creamer was the president of Brooklyn Ash Removal. In 1943 several of the larger homes in Allenhurst were leased to the United States Army Air Force Sub-Depot or Signal Corps. The Creamer home served as the company orderly room and mess hall for the enlisted men who were part of this special VHF (very high frequency) training program. The men gathered at 6:30 each morning on the beach in front of the Creamer house for calisthenics. The Borough also allowed the men to use the beach club and pool facilities. Following their training period and graduation these men were responsible for installing radar and VHF systems throughout the United States and Europe. (Lou Ellen Cohalan.)

Pictured in 1928 on the porch of 1 Spier Avenue are the following, from left to right: (seated) Hugh Skelley and Al Smith Jr.; (standing) Leonard Dean, Juliette Creamer, Martha Dean, Alfred Smith, Byron Creamer, Mrs. Smith, Judge John S. Walsh, Emily Walsh, Mrs. Al Smith Jr., and Fran Creamer. (Lou Ellen Cohalan.)

Capt. Wm. Rutledge Greer Jr. was among the 30 men assigned to the Army Air Force Signal Corps stationed at Allenhurst. Greer is pictured here around early 1940 in front of the temporary tent encampment at Fort Monmouth used to house the men until the accommodations at Allenhurst were ready. (Gerry Ann Greer Varley.)

The stately home at 106 Spier Avenue was built in the late 1890s and was featured in a pictorial of the 1930s called "Attractive Homes of New Jersey." At the time this photograph was taken the home was owned by Mrs. Eugene William Spaulding and was called "The Homestead." The home was remodeled in the mid-1940s and unbelievably the beautiful porte cochere and side porches were removed. (Randall Gabrielan.)

The entrance hall of the Spaulding home featured a fireplace with an elaborately carved mantle and tile work and beamed ceilings. Typical of most homes built in Allenhurst during this time, the entrance hall of the Spaulding home was large and welcoming. (Randall Gabrielan.)

Promoted as the "Rustic Bridge, Allenhurst, N.J." on a wide variety of postcards in the early 1900s, the wooden bridge that crossed over Deal Lake at the intersection of Spier Avenue and Lake Drive was the cause of much controversy. In 1913, a group of concerned residents appeared before the borough council to express their opinion that a new bridge be built, feeling the existing bridge was unsafe. However, James M. Ralston protested the building of a new bridge on what he believed to be part of his residential property. In 1916 the construction of a new bridge was in the works when Mr. Ralston filed suit, and the borough was ordered to appear before the New Jersey Supreme Court. Finally, in 1926, Ralston negotiated with the borough to relinquish his rights to the lake bank for the price of $18,000. In later years this part of the lake was filled in up to Lake Drive and the bridge was no longer required. (Allenhurst Centennial Committee.)

The building that now serves as the Allenhurst Borough Hall at the corner of Norwood and Corlies Avenues was originally the location of an early landmark called Grenelle & Schank's Ice Cream Parlor (later the Allenhurst Pharmacy). Many of the celebrities visiting the area in the summer months to perform in Asbury Park's hotels and stage establishments utilized the pharmacy. The fountain at the Allenhurst Pharmacy was the place to be seen on Saturday nights in the summer after the shows let out!

This is the Allenhurst Borough Hall as it appeared in a postcard mailed in 1957. In 1904 the borough purchased two lots on Hume Street, east of the power plant, for the purpose of building a firehouse and borough municipal building. In August of 1941, the administration of the borough was moved from the Hume Street location to its present location (shown above). (Robert Speck Collection.)

26

The Allenhurst Livery, also known as Buckelew & McCue's Livery, was in existence prior to the development of Allenhurst. It was located on Main Street close to the Deal border on Neptune Avenue. The livery provided boarding for horses as well as carriage maintenance. After 1925, it was used as a garage intermittently until a fire in 1940 caused damage to the structure; it was torn down shortly thereafter in response to complaints by residents. The post office was built on this site in 1958.

The Allenhurst Garage started operation in the early 1930s at 415 Main Street. In 1954 it was purchased by the Jersey Central Power & Light Company and incorporated into their existing operations. (Allenhurst Centennial Committee.)

A very early view of the Main Street business district depicts the John C. Conover Real Estate Agency, which was founded in 1906 and continues to operate from Allenhurst today. The post office operated from the Main Street location until 1960, when the new building was constructed on the site of the Buckelew & McCue Livery. (John C. Conover Agency.)

Prior to opening his own tailor shop on Main Street in 1910, P.H. Phillips worked at the Manhattan shops of the Brooks Brothers. (Allenhurst Centennial Committee.)

The Allenhurst Nurseries were owned and operated by Allenhurst developer James M. Ralston. The large hothouses and flower beds were located behind the Buckelew & McCue stables on Page Avenue. With the rapid development of the community, the nursery fulfilled the need for landscape plantings. The nursery property was sold in the 1930s to make way for residential housing.

The new post office was completed and dedicated in May 1960. The Allenhurst Post Office was established in a store front on Main and Hume Streets soon after the incorporation of the borough, with Mayor Benjamin wearing yet another hat as postmaster. Initially residents called for their mail at the post office until delivery service began in 1922. Prior to the establishment of the Allenhurst Post Office, mail for area residents came through the Deal Beach Post Office. (Allenhurst Centennial Committee.)

The Main Street business district had its start in 1895 when it included common purveyors such as a restaurant, blacksmith, grocer, and realtor. This postcard looking south, dated 1940, shows the Allenhurst National Bank and Trust Company (on the left), founded in 1926 by John C. Conover and Walter W. Reide Jr. The building remains today virtually unaltered as the offices of John C. Conover Realtors. (Robert Speck Collection.)

Prior to opening his market in the Plaza Building on Main Street in 1901, William Welshausen delivered fruits and vegetables from a horse-drawn cart to local residents. Before the start of World War II, the market was moved to the corner of Main and Corlies Avenues (as shown above). Mr. Welshausen enjoyed a good business assisted by his wife, Sophie, for 53 years, until he could no longer compete with the larger supermarkets. On February 11, 1954, the market held its last sale and never reopened. (Allenhurst Centennial Committee.)

Welshausen Market catered to the homeowners of Allenhurst and Interlaken in the early part of this century. Originally the market sold basic groceries and household staples, but as the community grew and the large homes became hosts for elegant dinner parties and teas, Mr. Welshausen sensed the need to upgrade his stock to include the "best imported and domestic wines."

The Schultz brothers, Martin, Ben and Carl, purchased both the Allenhurst and Deal Pharmacies in 1932. In 1942, the Allenhurst Pharmacy moved from the Norwood Avenue location to the Main Street business district, as seen here in this photograph from 1950. Following 40 years of business, the pharmacy was sold in 1972 to Samuel and Emanuel Jaffe. In 1992, a fire destroyed a large portion of the stores on this block and the pharmacy closed. (Alice Schultz.)

Martin and Alice Schultz, proprietors of the Allenhurst Pharmacy, are pictured here at the well-stocked smoke counter. The pharmacy also featured a soda fountain which was a popular stop for many shore residents following a Saturday night at the movies. (Alice Schultz.)

An early morning fire on April 1, 1976, destroyed several stores in the 400 block of the Main Street business district. (Randall Gabrielan.)

The Jane Logan Shop, located at 401 Spier Avenue during the 1950s and '60s, was a well-known eatery. It was succeeded by Arnst Card & Gift, which existed there until the early 1990s. (Allenhurst Centennial Committee.)

In 1898 the New York and Long Branch Railroad instituted a new stop at Allenhurst. The rapid growth of the community warranted the construction of the Allenhurst Depot on Main and Corlies Avenues. The cost to construct the classically styled stucco station was $15,388. In 1957 it was rumored that the NYLB Railroad was considering selling the depot to an independent concern planning to construct a shopping center. With the influence of the Homeowner's Association the station property was rezoned to restrict this type of construction. After failed attempts by the Allenhurst Preservation Committee to save the station, it was torn down in 1982. A small station exists behind the office building that is currently located on the site.

Railroad Park was originally the island created by the circular entrance to the Allenhurst Station. In 1905 the borough began leasing the property for $1 a year from the railroad company in order to maintain it as a park. After several years of negotiations, the borough purchased the property in 1950 for $12,000. (Courtesy Allenhurst Centennial Committee.)

Posing under the pergola in Railroad Park in 1926 are, from left to right, Gert Rogers, Sarah Speck, and Irene Rogers. (Robert Speck Collection.)

As part of the expansion of the Atlantic Coast Electric Railroad from Asbury Park northward to Pleasure Bay (part of Long Branch) in 1895 a 45-foot bridge was constructed across Deal Lake at Main Street for the exclusive use of the trolley lines. The bridge was designed and built by Robert Sloan of Asbury Park, who also built the elevated railroads in Chicago and New York City. (Joseph Eid Collection.)

On May 1, 1895, ground was broken for the large trolley car barn on Main Street. The building was considered the largest in Monmouth County at that time, with six entrance ways and a half-acre inside floor area designed to house 80 cars. The contractor for the project was S.W. Kirkbride. The property was purchased by JCP&L in 1931 and demolished in 1959 in order to provide additional parking. (Joseph Eid Collection.)

This is car #75 on its way into Asbury Park over the Deal Lake Bridge in 1915. The first trolley car to cross the new bridge departed from the Steinbach's store in Asbury Park at 5:45 p.m. on July 27, 1895. After crossing the bridge the car passed by the carbarn and power house in Allenhurst and then headed north passing through Deal on its way to the Elberon station. (Joseph Eid Collection.)

This photograph taken in 1915 shows car #211 outside the Allenhurst carbarn. In 1898 the fare from Asbury Park to Allenhurst, Interlaken, or Deal was 5¢. (Joseph Eid Collection.)

An aerial view of the Main Street trolley hub taken in 1923 clearly illustrates the location of the trolley barn, power house, and storage yard of the Atlantic Coast Electric Railroad.

Following the purchase of Allenhurst's electric light system in 1909, the Atlantic Coast Electric Light Company was competing with the Asbury Park Electric Company to provide both private and municipal lighting needs. In 1924, both the railway and electric company were reorganized. The electric company became the East Jersey Power Company. The trolley line

was combined with several other local companies to form the Coast Cities Railway Company. Over the course of the next several years, the trolley lines grew smaller and the buses of Coast Cities took their place. The facilities of the Eastern New Jersey Power Company were acquired by JCP&L in 1931 and have been modified to suit their operations over the years. (Joseph Eid Collection.)

Prior to 1895 the beach front was owned by Louie H. Ennis, who constructed a small open pavilion for use by bathers. This is a photograph of the original ocean pavilion built by the Coast Land Development Company as it appeared in 1898 just after it was constructed. (Monmouth County Historical Association.)

The original pavilion is shown here as seen from the beach. In 1901 the Borough purchased the beach and facilities for $63,000 from William Saxton and enlarged the existing wood-frame casino to include a second-story mezzanine overlooking the ocean. For the first 10 years the facilities were leased for management to the Allenhurst Realty Co. In 1913 the Borough took over complete operation of all beach facilities. (Monmouth County Historical Association.)

The interior of the original pavilion in 1898 was a gathering place, especially in the early part of the summer when cool ocean breezes provided relief from the heat. Edwin P. Benjamin, the founder of Allenhurst, provided free coach transportation from the train station to the beach pavilion for those visitors alighting at the Allenhurst station. In the early 1900s the wooden structure was torn down to make way for the new stucco casino. (Monmouth County Historical Association.)

This is a very early photograph of the second formal structure to occupy the beach front. The Allenhurst Casino was a classically styled two-story stucco structure designed by Ernest A. Arend of Asbury Park, and constructed by the I.R. Taylor Building Company. It featured an enclosed second story for those wishing to escape the elements, and down below the cool cement arches provided shade.

Minor changes were made to the casino in the early 1920s, including the addition of the unique bandstand and arched walkways. In 1924 a December northeaster that lasted for two days undermined the casino, causing significant settlement of the south end. In 1937, the pavilion was once again replaced. (Collection of John Rhody.)

This is Ocean Place as it appeared in the winter of 1933, looking toward the casino, with the original cement railings visible. (Allenhurst Centennial Committee.)

Frolicking on the Allenhurst boardwalk some time during the winter of 1933 are William Speck Sr. and Gertrude Rogers Speck. (Robert Speck Collection.)

This is an exterior shot of the SS *Allenhurst*. Construction began on the new nautical theme Allenhurst Casino in 1937. The "novel" design—as it was dubbed at that time—was the work of Ernest Arend, who had designed the previous stucco facilities.

A 1940s photograph of the beach facilities shows the lanai and concrete arches which were retained from the old stucco pavilion. Shuffleboard courts and restaurant seating have since taken the place of the manicured lawn and flower beds. The large pool in view is filled by saltwater from the Atlantic still to this day. (Allenhurst Centennial Committee.)

Following through on the nautical theme, authentic ship's railings were installed along the deck facing the ocean, and life boats complete with real rigging dangled above the beach. Two gangplanks provided access to the beach below. (Allenhurst Centennial Committee.)

The cabana colony located at the north end of the beach is pictured here in the early 1940s. The first discussions regarding the construction of cabanas began in the 1930s. Despite the fact that many residents expressed their objections, five double cabanas were constructed in 1933 adjacent to the sea wall. The cabanas have suffered severe damage and near destruction as a result of many coastal storms, requiring costly repairs through the years. (Allenhurst Centennial Committee.)

When the Allenhurst Police Department was established in 1898 officers were also obligated to report to fires within the borough. The photograph above depicts members of the police department taken during a dedication ceremony in 1970. They are, from left to right, Patrolmen Bates, Collins, Faulhaber, Ten Broeck, Chief Newman, Mayor McCaffrey, and Sgt. Dexter. (Allenhurst Police Department.)

Prior to the formation of its own fire department in 1898, the Borough of Allenhurst was paying the City of Asbury Park $15 per fire call. The above photograph shows four members of the crew in 1902, who were employed at a group rate of $50 per month beginning in 1901. (Collection John Rhody.)

The Hume Street fire house was built in 1901 by the issuance of a $22,000 bond. It was also at this time that the fire department was reorganized and 49 members were assigned badge numbers. George Allen was recorded as Badge No. 1. The firehouse also served as police headquarters for a short time prior to 1930. (Allenhurst Fire Department.)

The clubhouse and adjacent firehouse on Hume Street were demolished in 1997 to make way for modern facilities, scheduled to be completed in early 1998. (Allenhurst Fire Department.)

Located at the corner of Norwood and Elberon Avenues is the Episcopal Church of St. Andrew-by-the-Sea. Similar to most shore area churches, it was organized to serve the needs of summer visitors. Construction began on the church in 1891, following the finalization of a deed transferring the property from William E. Ford and Caro H. Ford of Morristown New Jersey. (Collection John Rhody.)

This is an interior view during service looking towards the altar. (Allenhurst Centennial Committee.)

The developers appreciated the importance of both the lake and the ocean as they related to the leisure activities of the borough's summer visitors. A 20-foot gravel roadway for access around the lake complete with a 5-foot-wide lover's lane was completed in the area west of the railroad tracks known as Benson Park.

An early view across the Hogswamp Creek portion of Deal Lake depicts Benson Park on the right, including the gazebo, also referred to as "the Summer House on the Lake."

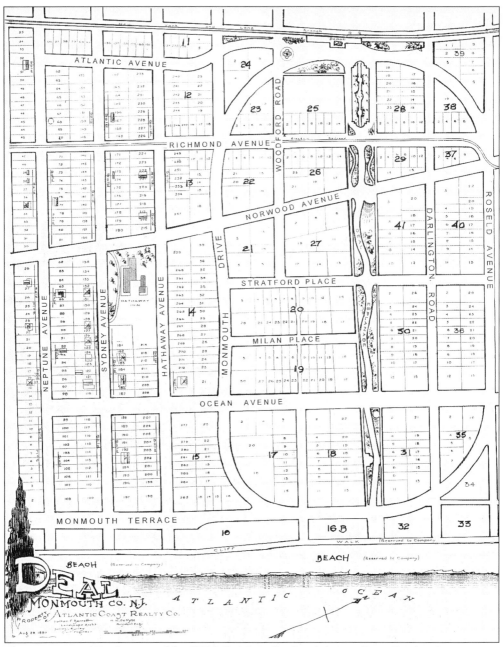

This is a map of Deal prepared by W.H. DeNyse for the Atlantic Coast Realty Company in August 1897. Many of the gentlemen involved in the realty company were also associated with the Atlantic Coast Electric Railway Company, which had just finished laying the trolley track to connect Asbury Park northward to Long Branch. The trolley route is shown on Richmond Avenue. The map includes a park-like plan for Deal Esplanade. Existing parcels north of Roseld Avenue are not shown. (Leon S. Avakian Associates.)

Two
The Borough of Deal

This is an image of the Thomas White homestead, believed to be one of the earliest residences established along the coast. It was constructed in 1768 in the area of present-day Deal Esplanade and Norwood Avenue. Thomas White (spelling changed from Whyte) was part of the long line of Whites who settled this area, having originally acquired land as far back as 1675 from Thomas Potter. (Ocean Township Historical Museum.)

The unique residence of Theodore S. Darling was built at 248 Ocean Avenue in the early 1900s. Darling, a business man from Asbury Park, erected the house, which was designed by architect Bradford Lee Gilbert of New York City in early 1900. Darling is attributed with the early development of the southern portion of Deal, which was known as Darlington from 1894 until 1897. The home exists today appearing slightly different due to renovations over the years. (William Temme.)

Darlington Station was built in 1894 on the plot of land that is just opposite the western end of Deal Esplanade. Visitors arriving at Deal Beach or Darlington would alight at this station and their first glimpse of the area would be the impressive Deal Esplanade. The structure was moved to the grounds of the Deal Golf & Country Club in 1902 when the new station was built on this site. (James Foley.)

The new railroad station was built in 1902. The construction of a new station at Long Branch in 1955 caused the Deal stop to be eliminated from the line. On February 15, 1958, the abandoned station was destroyed by fire.

Deal Esplanade was designed by landscape architect Nathan F. Barrett as the crowning feature of the community. Two formal gardens were situated at the ocean end and directly opposite Darlington Station. The perimeter of the avenue was trimmed with cedars, buttonballs, and scrub pines. Several seating areas provided peaceful views of the ocean from certain elevations. (Robert Speck Collection.)

A handsome cab is photographed on Deal Esplanade, probably some time between 1898 and 1900. In the background to the right a sign advertising land for sale by the Milan Ross Agency of Asbury Park is visible. (Landmark Realty.)

54

This is an early view of Sydney Avenue looking east towards Ocean Avenue. The residence of G.K. Thompson is included at the far end (see p. 63). (Robert Speck Collection.)

Similar to Deal Esplanade, Monmouth Road was part of the original land plan designed by Nathan F. Barrett in 1897. (Robert Speck Collection.)

116 Hathaway Inn, Deal, N. J.

In 1854, William Hathaway purchased the farm and hotel of Thomas Borden for $14,000. The structure was conveniently located on Deal Turnpike (Norwood Avenue) between Sydney and Hathaway Avenues. In 1897, it was the scene of a gala lawn party celebrating the incorporation of the Borough of Deal. It was torn down in 1933 following many years of solitude and neglect. (Robert Speck Collection.)

The Roseld Inn was originally located on Roseld Avenue at Roseld Court, on property located west of the first borough hall. At that time it was a small boarding house that accepted the overflow from the Hathaway Inn. Sometime around 1919, the inn was moved to the southwest corner of Neptune Avenue. It exists today as the Neptune Apartments. (Robert Speck Collection.)

The Deal Inn was located at 29 Richmond Avenue. Built in 1880, it was originally called the Deal Country Club Restaurant (no connection to Deal Golf & Country Club); later it became known as the Country Club Cafe. It closed in 1933 and the structure was destroyed by fire in October 1940. (Robert Speck Collection.)

The Hotel Banwright, located at 51 Hathaway Avenue, was one of the last establishments to accommodate guests staying in Deal well into the 1950s. The Banwright was strictly a summer establishment. It was destroyed by fire in 1960. (Robert Speck Collection.)

Miramare, the spectacular summer residence of Julia and Jefferson Seligman, was located at 191 Ocean Avenue. After acquiring the property in 1898, the mansion was completed in 1902. Jefferson was a partner in the firm J.W.Seligman from 1885 until he retired in 1935. Severely damaged by a fire in the late 1950s, the estate was torn down shortly after. (Long Branch Free Public Library.)

The magnificent estate of Henry Seligman was located on Ocean Avenue adjacent to the estate of Julia and Jefferson Seligman. The house featured a third-floor lanai from which to view the ocean. (Robert Speck Collection.)

The great estate of Isidor and Ida Straus was located on Ocean Avenue. The Straus's also owned property in Atlantic Highlands and Middletown. Mr. Straus was the president of the R.H. Macy Company and was often referred to as the "Merchant Prince" in the early part of this century. The house was razed in 1961 when Clem Conover Road was constructed. (James Foley.)

Mr. Isidor Straus (pictured here) and his wife, Ida, were among the many who perished in the sinking of the RMS *Titanic* in 1912. Mrs. Straus's devotion to her husband caused her to refuse several offers to board a lifeboat without Mr. Straus. Mr. Straus, being a gentlemen of the era, refused to board a boat until all the woman and children were safe. They were last seen walking away from the crowds arm in arm to await their fate.

This Mediterranean villa known as Sunny Haven was owned by Leo Sonneborn at the time this photograph was taken in 1911. Sonneborn owned an embroidery business in New York. The 27-room, 8-bath home was designed by H.A. Jacobs and constructed by the I.R. Taylor Building Company of Asbury Park. Located between the Durant and White estates on Ocean Avenue near Roseld Avenue, the home was sold in 1925 for $125,000. (Collection Long Branch Free Public Library.)

This is Raymere, the stately French-influenced mansion of General Motors founder William C. Durant. Originally built in 1908 by Jacob Rothschild, the 37-room, 14-bath home was located at Runyan and Ocean Avenues. Durant purchased the estate sometime around 1920 and lived there until 1940. In September of 1951, the Arnold Wrecking Company began the seven-week project to level the mansion. (Robert Speck Collection.)

In 1906, Edward V. Hartford, heir to the A&P fortune, commissioned the architectural firm of McKim, Mead & White to design his home at 217 Ocean Avenue. The Italian-style villa was situated on 3 acres and featured 20 rooms and a 5-car garage. Hartford dabbled with inventions related to the automobile and is credited with inventing and patenting the Hartford Shock Absorber. The home still exists today, but has been altered extensively. (Robert Speck Collection.)

A butler awaits the arrival of dinner guests in the formal dining room of the Hartford estate, *c.* 1934.

BROOKSIDE, DEAL, N. J.

"Brookside," the home of J.C. Lee, president of Monmouth Shirt Company, was located at the northwest corner of Poplar and Ocean Avenues. (Robert Speck Collection.)

"CLARADEN," HOME OF ARTHUR LIPPER, DEAL, N. J.

The home of Arthur Lipper, located on the southwest corner of Brighton and Ocean, was known as Claraden. (Robert Speck Collection.)

The landmark tudor chalet located on Sydney and Ocean was designed by its owner, architect G.K. Thompson, in 1897. Thompson also designed several buildings in New York City, including the Standard Oil Building, the Manhattan Life Building, and the B. Altman & Company building. Unfortunately, the home was severely damaged by fire in the early spring of 1997 and was razed later that year. (Landmark Realty.)

The estate of Newman Erb, built in 1903, covered almost an entire block from Roosevelt Avenue to Ocean Avenue, and south to Poplar and Norwood Avenue. Poplar Brook ran through the rear of the property. Mr. Erb's estate was well known for its beautiful vistas, immaculate landscaping, and exotic gardens. The home was designed by architect Clarence W. Luce.

The mansion of Arthur Horgan was located on Deal Esplanade opposite Darlington Station. The stately brick home was built in 1904, and was designed by Carrere & Hastings, a New York architectural firm who designed homes for the very wealthy. In 1913, Frederick Sperman purchased the property from Horgan's estate. The mansion had a colorful existence. In the 1920s it was a nightclub called the Braxton Club, which was known in certain circles for its abundance of spirits as well as gambling entertainment. It was also a restaurant called DeLisle's in 1925. In 1932 it was purchased by Donald Unterman, who established the Deal Conservatoire of Arts and Theater. The conservatoire was well-received initially; however, interest waned and the establishment closed in mid-1940. The building was torn down in 1955 and is the site of four residences today. (Robert Speck Collection.)

Deal Conservatoire of Arts and Theatre

Presents

"GOLDILOCKS and the THREE BEARS"

A Children's Operetta

Direction---Rose Ludlum

ALSO

DANCE RECITAL

Direction---Mabel Parish

Friday, June 7th, at 8:00 P. M.

Admission 50 Cents

Saturday, June 8th, at 2:15 P. M.

Adults 50 Cents   Children 25 Cents

Deal Conservatoire Theatre

Deal Esplanade, Deal, N. J.

BENEFIT OF BOY SCOUTS, TROOP 66

The conservatoire featured a large array of professional and amateur talents. This program from a 1941 production was a benefit for a local boy scout troop. The conservatoire also ran a summer theater series which provided a theatrical and artistic outlet for local youngsters during summer recess. (Robert Speck Collection.)

Mrs. C. Kaye named her Greek Revival-styled home Arcadia. It was located at the northwest corner of Brighton and Ocean Avenue. (Monmouth County Historical Association.)

This is a rear view of Arcadia. (Monmouth County Historical Association.)

The front porch of Arcadia faced Ocean Avenue and provided a sweeping view across the front lawn to the ocean. In 1907 a new casino was built across the street from the residence. Following a public auction to dispose of the interior elements, the structure was razed in 1987 before a large audience. (Monmouth County Historical Association.)

Pictured above, the main parlor featured an indoor fountain and fish pond. The ballroom and dining room contained original silk panels and other wall ornamentation acquired from the Vanderbilt mansion in Manhattan prior to its demolition. (Monmouth County Historical Association.)

The first borough hall was located on the northwest corner of Monmouth Drive and Norwood Avenue. The building also served as the police station and jail. The building and property was sold at auction in October 1939 for $15,000. (Robert Speck Collection.)

This is a very early photograph of the new borough hall when it was still under construction in 1924. The unique brick tudor structure is situated at the corner of Roseld and Norwood Avenues on property that was donated by William C. and Catherine Durant. The building remains today as the borough municipal offices and police station.

Soon after its incorporation in June 1898, Deal's first mayor William H. Appleton appointed three men to serve in the capacity of "special policemen." These men were Frank Bartholomew, Lewis Havens, and Peter Combs. In July of 1899, John Carroll became the fourth officer. In 1902, the growth of the borough warranted hiring a fifth officer, Frank Rogers Sr. Two years later, Rogers was appointed the first chief marshall of Deal by Mayor William Hogancamp. In the photograph above, taken outside the original borough hall in early 1900, Frank Rogers is seated second from the left. Rogers served as chief of police until the time of his death in 1936. (Robert Speck Collection.)

These borough police officers posed *c.* 1946 in front of the entrance to the borough hall. From left to right they are as follows: (front row) Dominick Torchia, Chief John Rehm, and Stanley Conover; (back row) Stuart Sevine, John Anderson, Joseph Stronanger, and William Speck. (Robert W. Speck Collection.)

Deal Fire Company No. 1 was organized in 1911; however, due to unspecified reasons, it disbanded soon after. In this photograph, taken in 1911, the members of Deal Fire Company No. 1 pose in front of a new Webb Pumper engine. It was the first motorized pumper in use in New Jersey. (Robert Speck Collection.)

DEAL FIRE COMPANY, No. 2

DEAL FIRE ALARM SIGNALS

To give an alarm by Telephone, first call 1000 Deal and give exact location of fire. The alarm will then be turned in from Headquarters to the nearest box.

6 Deal Fire House	25 Parker and Norwood	43 Monm'th & Norw'd
12 Lawrence and Ocean	26 Runyon and Ocean	45 Monm'th and Atlan.
13 Jerome and Pleasant	31 Roseld and Norwood	46 Hathaway & Ocean
14 Almyr and Pearl	32 Darlington and Ocean	51 Sydney & Norwood
15 Pearl and Ocean	34 Deal Esp. and Atlan.	52 Ocean and Neptune
16 Norwood and Morgan	35 Surf and Ocean	53 Atlan. and Neptune
21 Poplar and Ocean	36 Stratf'd & Deal Esp.	3 Fire Out
23 Phillips and Norwood	41 Woodf'd & Richm'd	
24 Brighton and Ocean	42 Deal Casino	

Out of Town Calls
54 North
56 South
1 Test
2 12 o'clock noon
2 Following Box No.— Second Alarm
7 General Alarm

★

Telephone 2817

A. MATOVSKY
FLORIST
DEAL, NEW JERSEY

Deal Fire Company No. 2 was sanctioned and organized in 1912. It was at this same time that construction of the Brighton Avenue firehouse began. The members of Fire Company No. 2 appear on this call card sponsored by Matovsky Florist during the 1940s. (Courtesy James Foley.)

Venison Dinner
Tendered
Theodore H. Beringer
President of Deal Fire Co. N°2

The above photo is a traditional group shot taken in 1935 at Gene Tinelli's Restaurant in Elberon during a dinner honoring Theodore H. Beringer, president of Deal Fire Company No. 2. Mr. Beringer also served as a borough councilman from 1914 to 1960. (Robert Speck Collection.)

Club House, Deal Beach., N. J.

The development of the Deal "golf links" can be attributed to the social development of Deal Beach. In 1895, financier George Washington Young visited the shore area and selected 135 acres in the western portion of the tract to establish his residence. He also commissioned Lawrence Van Etten to design a nine-hole golf course for his private use. At the suggestion of close friend and business associate J. Henry Haggerty, he established a private club. In 1898 the course was doubled in size to an 18-hole course stretching over 7,000 yards. In that same year the club was incorporated as the Deal Golf Club. Among the honorary memberships in that first year were President William McKinley, Vice President Garret A. Hobart, and former president Benjamin Harrison. The clubhouse pictured above was constructed in 1898 as a one-story building intended for summer use only. In 1903, the second story was added. The clubhouse remains to this day a very important part of the club's heritage. (Robert Speck Collection.)

When the new railroad station was constructed in 1902, the club organizers bid on the old Darlington station to serve as the men's locker facilities. The building was moved in that same year to the grounds of the golf course. In 1962, new locker facilities were constructed. (Deal Golf & Country Club Archives.)

This aerial photograph taken in 1973 depicts a large portion of the present layout of the 18-hole course. Prior to 1914 the fourth, fifth and sixth holes were located on the northwest side of Roseld Avenue. Due to financial reasons, club owner Young sold property on the eastern side of Roseld Avenue, including the three holes, to the Hollywood Golf Club. The course was modified utilizing land on the western part of Monmouth Road. (Deal Golf & Country Club.)

The above photograph depicts a group of golfers taken at the Deal Country Club in the 1920s. Unfortunately not all the names of the gentlemen in this snazzy group are known. First on left is Dr. Harold V. Garrity Sr. (a 14-time club champion), Theodore F. Appleby Jr. is standing third from the left, and Dr. James A. Fisher Sr. is the second man from the right. (Deal Golf & Country Club.)

In 1899, a short nine-hole course was designed and constructed for the exclusive use of the 44 female members of the club. In 1900 there were deliberations over allowing woman to play on the "long course" and a decision was made to allow "Ladies to Play" on Monday afternoons. In August of 1900, 22 women members were granted associate memberships. (Deal Golf & Country Club.)

George W. Young built this rustic bungalow off Roseld Avenue as a wedding gift for his new wife, Madame Lillian Nordica, in 1910. The hundreds of guests attending the housewarming party were entertained by an orchestra, Neapolitan singers, and a Russian ballet troupe. Many of the guests who attended from New York were carried by a private railcar chartered specifically for the occasion. (Moss Archives.)

Prior to marrying George W. Young in 1909, Madame Lillian Nordica traveled throughout Europe and the United States performing at many prestigious opera houses. In 1913, Madame Nordica became ill while on a concert tour. She died in 1914 at Batavia, Java. But for a few small shared holdings, a newly executed will excluded her husband. (Karen Schnitzpahn.)

Without question, the most magnificent residence to be built along Deal Lake was the Tudor mansion of Daniel O'Day, a prominent figure in the early development of the Standard Oil Company. To celebrate the completion of his estate, known as "Kildysart," in 1902, O'Day hosted an intimate lawn party for a rumored 2,000 guests. Entertainment was also on the grand scale, and the 69th Regiment Band of New York City played until the early hours of the morning. Among the many prestigious figures in attendance at the event was former president Grover Cleveland. The estate was accessed by a handsome brick bridge off Atlantic Avenue. O'Day died in 1906 in France at the age of 62. (Paul Imgrund & Ann Steen.)

The estate was purchased in 1914 by William P. Ahnelt, publisher and owner of *Pictorial Review* magazine. It became known as "Ahnelt Hall." Mr. Ahnelt and his wife, Suzanne, are pictured here enjoying a spring afternoon in the wildflower fields along with their dog and a young Ann Imgrund, the daughter of their loyal estate assistants, Herman and Lina Imgrund. (Imgrund & Steen.)

Directly behind the tennis courts on the estate were the large hot houses. The Ahnelts kept a collection of tropical plants (including lemon and orange trees) and exotic birds here (the birds were allowed to fly freely throughout). Several pools were located throughout the greenhouse stocked with goldfish. The greenhouse was attached to the main house by an awning covered walkway. (Imgrund & Steen.)

The Imgrunds occupied one half of this duplex dwelling on the estate year round while the other half was used to accommodate the temporary help hired for the summer months such as gardeners and carpenters. This structure remains today as a single-family residence in Deal Harbor Estates. (Imgrund & Steen.)

Paul and Ann Imgrund were both born on the estate and grew up there as well. They are pictured in 1929 on the swing set fashioned for them near the car garage. (Imgrund and Steen.)

Herman Otto Imgrund, the Ahnelt's auto mechanic and chauffeur, is seen in this 1920 photograph posing between two slaughtered sows. The estate had its own slaughterhouse and smokehouse for processing livestock. (Imgrund and Steen.)

These are some of the automobiles in Ahnelt's fleet, all of which were maintained by Mr. Imgrund. Ahnelt Hall was destroyed by an early morning fire in June 1935. The community of Deal Harbor estates was developed on the former estate grounds in the late 1950s. (Imgrund and Steen.)

Photographed in early 1900 are borough water sprinkler wagons in front of the entrance to the estate on Atlantic Avenue. Water sprinkling was a common practice before paved roads in order to minimize the disturbance of dust on the roadways. Water sprinkler trucks also served as early fire tankers when necessary. Police Chief Frank Rogers appears in uniform on the center wagon. (Robert Speck Collection.)

This view from the tower of Ahnelt Hall was taken in 1924 looking out over Richmond Avenue. St. Mary's Church is visible in the center of the photograph. The estate's original owner, Daniel O'Day, donated property and pledged matching funds up to $10,000 for the construction of a church. The response was good and in 1904 the construction of St. Mary's began. (Imgrund and Steen.)

At the close of the summer season of 1900, a group of seasonal residents approached Reverend M.L. Glennon of the Holy Spirit parish in Asbury Park to discuss the possibility of conducting a mass at a location in Deal. In June of the following year, a surprising number of people attended the first mass held at the Hathaway Inn, conducted by Reverend Crean of St. Michael's Church in West End. As the informal congregation grew, it became necessary to conduct the masses in a tent that had been set up on a vacant lot between Richmond and Atlantic Avenues. The "Canvas Church of Deal" continued through the summer of 1902. Prior to the completion of the stone church in 1905, a roof was extended over the basement and services were moved there. The rectory as seen to the left was completed in 1906. (Collection John Rhody.)

The Deal Casino, built between 1906 and 1907, was originally located on Ocean Avenue. It was razed in March of 1958 and is now a residential section of the borough. A new casino, which still exists today, was built a few blocks north on Ocean Avenue in 1957. (Collection Randall Gabrielan.)

Al Woolman (left) sits watch c. 1921 with his partner, Ridgeway Pyott, on the beach at the original Deal Casino. (Robert Speck Collection.)

A 1938 scene of the old Deal Casino depicts an unusual sight of canoes navigating the adult pool. (Robert Speck Collection.)

This interior view of the original casino on an obviously crowded day in 1947 shows the enormous adult and children's pools. (Robert Speck Collection.)

These very "mod" Deal Casino beach huts were constructed in the late 1960s, following a storm which destroyed the original bath houses in 1965. (Robert Speck Collection.)

The Deal Casino, as it appears today, plays host to a membership of over 5,000 during the summer months.

Pictured on the grounds of the Deal Casino looking toward Marine Place in 1944 are, from left to right, Gertrude Speck, Leslie Potter (manager of the Deal Casino for over 40 years), Clara Hazelrigg (assistant manager of the Phillips Avenue Beach Club), John Rehm (chief of police), and Robert Kleine (manager of the Phillips Avenue Beach Club). The original Phillips Avenue Casino was built on the north side of Phillips Avenue Pier south of the Seligman estates. A coastal storm in 1935 caused extensive damage to the original pavilion and bathhouses. (Robert Speck Collection.)

The spirit of summer—sun, surf, and fun is reflected in this 1932 portrait of young ladies taken at the Old Phillips Avenue Beach. They are, from left to right, Dorothy Rehm, Francis Sevine, Margaret Dunn, and Marie Sevine. (Margaret Dunn.)

These young boys were photographed on the beach at Phillips Avenue c. 1928. (Robert Speck Collection.)

In 1960, Hurricane Donna skirted the coast by 100 miles; however, the winds were sufficient enough to cause damage in many coastal communities. The photograph above shows a local resident surveying the damage at the Phillips Avenue beach and pier the morning after. (Robert Speck Collection.)

The new Phillips Avenue beach pavilion was built in 1936 to replace the previous facilities damaged by a storm the year prior. In 1995 the pavilion was renamed the "W. Stanley Conover Pavilion" in honor of Mr. Conover who served the borough for over 40 years in many capacities."

A photograph taken in 1937 shows the California Produce Market that was located on Phillips Avenue at the southwest corner of Norwood Avenue. The market was also called the American Market for a short time. (Robert Speck Collection.)

This photograph, taken in 1938, records the existence of Deal Center, a commercial building located at 2 Ocean Avenue owned by Charles Sacco. It was located on Lawrence and Ocean Avenue. Among the many establishments to lease space was the Oxford Restaurant. In the early 1990s the property was sold and the building razed. (Robert Speck Collection.)

It must have been a Sunday, for these boys appear too well dressed to be stopping in for sodas at the Deal Soda Shop on just any day in 1922. The Deal Soda Shop was located in the Norwood Avenue block of stores, the site of the present-day Falafel shop. From left to right the boys are Bill Speck, Richard Woods, and Bob Fisher. (Robert Speck Collection.)

Following World War II, the citizens of Deal, NJ, provided financial aid to the residents of their sister city—Deal, County of Kent, England—enabling them to rebuild their severely damaged community. In August of 1976, John Alvery (right), the mayor of Deal, England, accompanied by his wife, Katheline, visited the United States and presented the key to their city to then mayor of Deal Daniel Kruman along with his wife, Charlotte. (Collection Randall Gabrielan.)

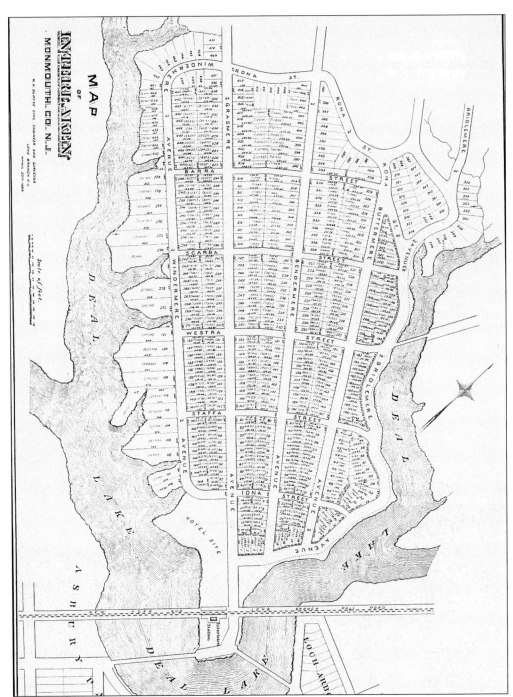

This map of Interlaken prepared in 1889 depicts the entire community as originally planned. The far western end was not developed until after 1920 and does not appear. With the exception of Bridlemere, the east and west avenues ending in "mere" are named after lakes in England's northern district. The cross streets—Iona, Staffa, Westra, Scarba, Barra, and Rona—are names drawn from the Scottish Islands of the Hebrides in the Irish Sea. (Elizabeth Couse.)

Three

The Borough of Interlaken

Interlaken Farm was established by Dr. Francis M. Weld and his wife, Fannie, in 1888. The Boston natives purchased the 364 acres along with a farmhouse and outbuildings from the heirs of Peter Drummond, an early settler in this area. Following a brief attempt to raise cattle, Dr. Weld formed the Interlaken Land Development Company in 1890, and plans for a residential community were launched. The farmhouse, which was located on Wickapecko Drive just about where Darlene Avenue is today, was destroyed by a fire on Halloween night 1933.

The initial attempt to establish the community of Interlaken by Dr. Weld and his associates failed due to strict building codes specifying the construction of large dwellings only. The property was then passed to the International Trust Company of Boston in 1905, who hired the management firm of Stormfeltz-Loveley-Neville Company to continue the building efforts. As part of their new vision for Interlaken Park, they constructed the stately stone gates at the eastern entrance on Grasmere Avenue.

In this early 1900 photograph these lovely young ladies found the gates a suitable location for a group shot. Interlaken Park was located just beyond the gates to the north, and a walkway which once existed along the lake's shore on Bridlemere Avenue was a popular strolling lane. Today this area has been developed into an arboretum by the Interlaken Shade Tree Commission. (Ocean Grove Historical Society.)

The Interlaken Train Station was constructed as a result of Ocean Grove's charter restrictions which did not allow trains to stop within one mile of the community on Sundays. This restriction applied to the new Asbury Park and Ocean Grove stations. In order to accommodate those passengers wishing to visit the new resort community of Asbury Park, this stone station was built *c.* 1889 just east of where the entrance gates stand today.

These folks are awaiting the train's arrival at Interlaken Station early in 1890. With the appeal of the Ocean Grove restrictions in 1912, the station was no longer needed in light of additional stations at Allenhurst and North Asbury Park. It was torn down that same year. (Interlaken Library Collection.)

The cottage of Andrew J. Dam, Esq., located on the northwest corner of Grasmere and Bridlemere Avenues, was one of the first four homes built in Interlaken after the subdivision of the property.

Windermere Avenue follows Romaine's Creek, a tributary along the Deal Lake. The shady nooks and inlets along the lake made Windermere Avenue one of the more desirable locations for home construction. In addition, lakefront lots were generally larger, allowing for separate structures such as boathouses and studios.

Interlaken's original developers, a group of physicians from New York and Boston, proposed the construction of a magnificent Tudor-style hotel. A map of the community on p. 90 shows a large area of land designated as "hotel site" at the eastern end of Grasmere Avenue. The Interlaken Inn never materialized past this artist's rendering that appeared in the 1895 prospectus.

To this day Interlaken remains a strictly residential community. However, Erv Slover's Service Station (as pictured here in 1926) can be awarded the honor of being the closest thing to a business Interlaken has ever seen. Located just outside the gates in the vicinity of the old train station, the tiny garage was torn down in 1944. (Charlie & Lil Slover.)

The structure that served as the first Interlaken Borough Hall, beginning in 1922, was originally constructed and used by the Stormfeltz-Loveley-Neville Company as a sales office in 1906. The tiny one-room concrete building was torn down in 1958 to make way for the new building. This photograph was taken just prior to demolition by lifelong Interlaken resident and historian Fritz Cleary.

Designed by local architect David Marner, the new borough hall was dedicated on November 9, 1958. It continues to be the social hub of Interlaken, and houses the police station, court house, and library. (Interlaken Library Collection.)

Interlaken has been fortunate to have many local residents dedicated to the continuing growth and well being of the borough. Pictured here are, from left to right, Police Chief Frank Cowley (who served the borough a total of 29 years), Sanford C. Flint (who served the borough as a councilman for 16 years and as mayor for 24 years, for a total dedication of 40 years), and Robert H. Adams (who held the position of borough clerk for 50 years, from 1927 until 1977). (Interlaken Library Collection.)

Interlaken's finest c. 1945 are, from left to right, Joseph Brown, William Hankinson, Chief Frank Cowley, and Milt Johnson. This group represents quite a genesis from Interlaken's first police officer, James Parker, who patrolled the borough on a bicycle for a salary of $100 per month. (Robert Todd.)

This is the back of a souvenir postcard promoting the 1910 air meet sponsored by the Aero and Motor Club of Asbury Park. The meet was held in an open field on the western outskirts of Interlaken on Wickapecko Drive, where the recreation field is located today. The event culminated on August 27, 1910, following a series of fascinating stunts and also one tragedy.

In this image a biplane of the era soars over the field. Following the accidental crash landing of his craft, Walter Brookins sustained minor injuries as did several of those seated in the large grandstand. Two days later, Benny Prinz, a parachutist aboard a hot air balloon, fell to his death after loosing his footing. (George Cook Jr.)

A group of aviation enthusiasts listen intently as Wilbur Wright (far left) appears to be explaining something to the group. In regard to the death of Prinz, Wright later commented that winds of 25 miles per hour were not conducive to flying that day. Contrary to rumored accounts, neither of the Wright brothers flew at this meet. (George Cook Jr.)

Behind the controls are Governor Fort (left) and aviator Archibald Hoxsey of Pasadena, California. Hoxsey was killed a month later while performing at a show in Los Angeles. (George Cook Jr.)

This is a photograph of "Pine Cove," built by Interlaken's first mayor, Frank Stick, at 510 Windermere Avenue in 1924. Stick was a pioneer naturalist and wildlife illustrator who had studied under Howard Pyle—the dean of American illustrators—before coming to Interlaken. (David Stick.)

Stick built his studio overlooking the lake as shown in this image from 1925. From this peaceful location he created an enormous amount of illustrations depicting every type of wildlife imaginable. His work appeared in a variety of publications, including *Sports Afield*, *Redbook*, *Field & Stream*, *Collier's*, *Harper's*, and the *Saturday Evening Post*. (Photograph by Francis X. Cleary.)

David Stick, the son of Frank Stick, provided this charming 1928 photograph of he and two of his buddies fishing on the floating dock that his dad built on the lake. David is the young man sitting on the log in the forefront.

This image of Frank Stick appeared in a 1924 edition of *Outdoor America*. In 1922, Stick finished his last two commissioned illustrations for *Ladie's Home Journal* and vowed to never paint for pay again. In 1929 he and his family moved to a remote section of North Carolina and he continued to paint for pleasure. Stick died in 1966 at the age of 82. (David Stick.)

In 1917, the residence at 86 Grasmere Avenue was purchased by western artist William Henry David Koerner, professionally known as W.H.D. Koerner. Koerner was coaxed into moving to Interlaken by his friend and fellow artist Frank Stick, who was already settled in the area. With the addition of two skylights and a potbelly stove, the carriage house at the rear of the property was used as the artist's studio.

Later, in 1919, Koerner designed a freestanding studio facing Grasmere Avenue adjacent to the house. Lillian and Bill Koerner are shown here in this photograph taken in 1928 on the steps of the studio. Lillian was the guardian of her husband's privacy, standing watch at the kitchen window to keep uninvited guests away when deadlines were closing in on the busy artist. (Ruth Koerner Oliver.)

Koerner created hundreds of huge canvases depicting life in the western United States during the Golden Era of magazine illustration. These paintings were most often commissioned for serial publications such as *McClure's*, *Redbook*, *Collier's*, the *Saturday Evening Post*, and *Ladie's Home Journal* to name a few. The studio was also used for entertaining friends on Saturday nights when the freshly waxed floors would be lined with candles and the Victrola brought over from the house. The artist's health began to fail and in 1938 he died at the age of 58. A memorial service was held in the Grasmere Avenue studio, where Koerner was surrounded by his favorite works selected by Lillian. In 1978, an interior replica of Koerner's Interlaken studio was dedicated as a permanent exhibit at the Buffalo Bill Historical Center, Whitney Gallery of Western Art in Cody, Wyoming. (Ruth Koerner Oliver.)

William Percy Couse pictured here in 1939 came to Interlaken as a young illustrator in 1922. He was introduced to Elizabeth Meares, daughter of Harper's Magazine Editor, William Ellis Meares at the home of Bill and Lillian Koerner that same year. In 1924, they were married and established residence in Interlaken, adding yet another artist to the growing community. (Elizabeth Couse.)

The Couse residence at 615 Grasmere Avenue was originally constructed in 1924 primarily as a studio with living quarters upstairs. The home underwent several renovations upwards as the Couse family grew. William's sister, Emily Couse Birdsall, was also an artist who settled in Interlaken, establishing a studio at 711 Bendermere Avenue. (Elizabeth Couse.)

The house at 209 Windermere Avenue was built in 1913, and was designed by its original owner, Katherine Walsh, a painter and architect. Lifetime resident Fritz Cleary was born in the house in 1914. Cleary, the grandson of Katherine Walsh, spent his summers in Interlaken until the age of 13, when he moved to Interlaken permanently. (Hope Cleary.)

This is a very early portrait of Fritz Cleary taken along Deal Lake in 1924. Fritz went on to graduate from St. John's University and the National Academy of Design in New York City. He was a very talented sculptor, as well as a journalist with the *Asbury Park Press* for 32 years. He was also a teacher and supporter of the Fine Arts Museum in Asbury Park and a general advocate of the arts and education throughout Monmouth County. In the early 1960s, Cleary purchased the Koerner home and studio on Grasmere Avenue and worked there for 30 years. He passed away in 1993 at the age of 80. (Hope Cleary.)

Representing one of Interlaken's largest examples of English Tudor architecture, this distinguished home is located on the Deal Lake at 408 Windermere Avenue. It was designed by Frank Cole of Asbury Park at the request of Oliver K. Parry and Carol Ackerman Parry shortly after their marriage in 1927. Construction was completed in 1929. (Parry Family.)

Oliver K. Parry and Carol Ackerman are pictured here in 1931 along the Deal Lake behind their home. Following the completion of his medical degree from New York University in 1923, Parry came to the shore area at the request of Dr. James F. Ackerman of Asbury Park. Dr. Parry was a well-respected surgeon in the shore area. Mrs. Parry was the daughter of Dr. Ackerman. (Parry Family.)

This rare real photograph postcard of "Windermere Cottage" was mailed on June 18, 1922, just days before Interlaken was incorporated. Originally built by Ms. Theresa Horan in approximately 1906, the three-story home was designed by Ernest A. Arend, a prominent architect who designed many private homes and beach pavilions throughout the area.

Interlaken seems to have more than its fair share of Tudors. This home located on 204 Grasmere was built in the early part of this century. In 1920 it was purchased by Wilson G. Hunt of Jersey City, and it served as a summer home for his family. This photograph, taken in 1931, shows the family's Pierce Arrow parked in front of the house. (Parry Family.)

The large colonial at 612 Grasmere Avenue was built by J. Otto Rhome in 1922. This photograph, taken in 1925, shows the formal gardens and fish pond located on the south side of the home. A clay tennis court was also located on the property. In 1936 the 3-acre lot was subdivided into two additional building lots. The Rhome family occupied the home until 1937. (John O. Rhome Jr.)

J. Otto Rhome was born on April 10, 1878, in Santarem, Brazil. His family was among the many southerners that migrated to Brazil following the Civil War with the promise of inexpensive and abundant land. He returned to the United States in 1886 to attend school. Rhome, an attorney by profession, was also involved in land investment, playing a large role in the development of Interlaken. (John O. Rhome Jr.)

This lovely portrait was taken in 1924 and depicts John O. Rhome Jr. and his sister, Gwenyth, seated next to the fish pond shown in the photo at left. John Jr. attended Princeton University and pursued a career in law similar to his father, while his sister attended Wellesley College, similar to her mother, Ethel Morgan Rhome. (John O. Rhome Jr.)

Directly across the street from the Rhome's residence was another large home, built in 1929 by Mr. and Mrs. Robert A. Tusting, owners of Tusting Piano Company in Asbury Park, the shore's oldest music company (founded in 1883). As a note of interest, a scaled-down replica of this house exists at the corner of Windermere Avenue and Staffa Street.

Construction began on the home at 300 Bridlemere Avenue in 1890 and took a little over a year to complete. It was built by Charles H. Thomas, whose son, Kenneth C. Thomas, was the author of several novels published early in the twentieth century. As Interlaken experienced enormous growth in the early 1920s—due in part to the influx of writers, artists, and actors—the Thomas house became an unofficial clubhouse for the more creative of Interlaken's residents.

An early view of the home at 21 Rona under construction in 1924 also shows the one house that existed on Raymere Avenue at this time. The home was built by Sanford Flint, longtime Interlaken mayor, who lived there until 1986. (Joyce Barrett.)

INTERLAKEN

Asbury Park's Most Beautiful Residential Section

INTERLAKEN DEVELOPMENT COMPANY

REPRESENTED BY

PHONE ASBURY PARK { 4394 3418 543

The majority of the homes that exist in Interlaken today were built between the period of 1920 through 1935. Many early residents purchased several lots on which to build their homes and later realized they could sell these lots for a nice profit. This is a business card from the Interlaken Development Company, organized in the 1920s by a group of residents selling miscellaneous lots throughout the borough. (Interlaken Library Collection.)

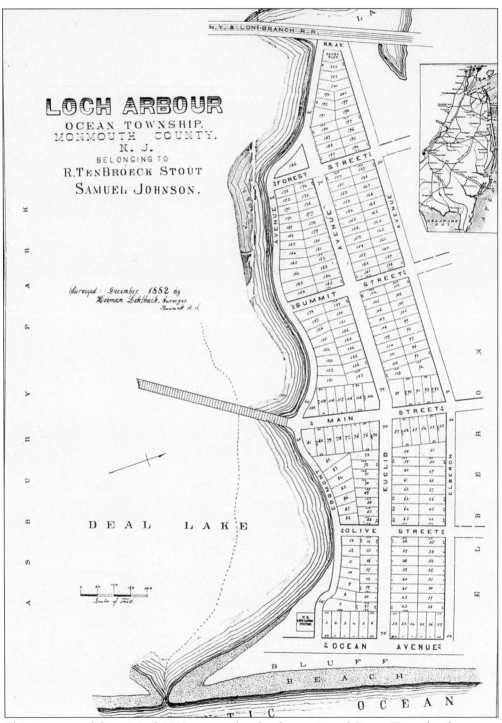

This is a copy of the original 1882 survey plan for the section of Ocean Township known as Loch Arbour. "Loch Arbour," meaning "lake in the forest," was taken from the name that Gavin Drummond, an early settler in this area, gave to the Great Pond, which is today known as Deal Lake. (Moss Archives.)

One
The Village of
Loch Arbour

Mary and Edward Boyle purchased this structure, along with 65 acres bordering Great Pond (Deal Lake) and the ocean, in 1864. It is believed that the cottage was moved from its original location to the west side of Deal Turnpike (Norwood Avenue) in close proximity to the old wooden bridge over Great Pond. Following the sudden death of the Boyles in 1881, the property was purchased by Samuel Johnson and R. Tenbroeck Stout for $110,000. (Collection Long Branch Free Public Library.)

The Deal Beach Life Saving Station was among the first eight stations established in 1849. Abner Allen was the official wreckmaster. The original station, which was nothing more than a simple shack to house the appropriated supplies, was located at the inlet from the ocean just north of Deal Lake in present-day Loch Arbour. The new station (at left) was built around 1884, after additional funding was provided to the service. (Robert Speck Collection.)

The surfmen of the Deal beach Life Saving Station are shown here in the late 1890s proudly posing with their surf boats, which were designed to navigate rough seas during a storm. In 1915, when the U.S. Coast Guard was established, this station was designated as Deal No. 6. (Robert Speck Collection.)

This is a portrait of Edwin Stanton Patterson taken in 1918. Mr. Patterson served as a member of the crew at the Deal Station from approximately 1915 to 1918. (Robert Speck Collection.)

This photograph of the lifesaving crew of Deal Station No. 6 was taken in 1914 just prior to the union of the Revenue Cutter Service and the Life Saving Service to form the U.S. Coast Guard in 1915. Deal Station No. 6 was demolished in the late 1940s. (Robert Speck Collection.)

This 1902 photograph shows the union of many crossings over the Deal Lake. The trolley bridge in the center was built in 1895 and ran almost parallel to the Main Street vehicular bridge constructed in 1894. The original wooden bridge into Loch Arbour runs on the diagonal. The canopy of a boat livery is visible in the bottom of the image.

This picturesque view across Deal Lake shows Edgemont Drive up to the Park Avenue Bridge. The original entrance into Loch Arbour was an old wooden bridge that crossed Deal Lake diagonally from the Interlaken Railroad station to where the Thompson Livery Stable was located at Main and Euclid Avenue on the Loch Arbour side. (Ann Steen.)

An aerial view of Deal Lake taken in the early 1920s shows the majority of Loch Arbour in the right corner. Still a part of Ocean Township at this time, Loch Arbour was the only part of the township that was actually on the ocean. In the distance the Atlantic Coast Electric Railroad trolley bridge crossing the Deal Lake can be seen running parallel to the Main Street bridge. Note the appearance of Interlaken as heavily wooded with an occasional roof top poking through. (Peter Lucia.)

This is a popular postcard view showing some of the most elegant homes in Loch Arbour's residential section along Edgemont Drive facing the Deal Lake.

Mr. and Mrs. Walter J. Raleigh and their children pose in 1931 at the boat dock on Edgemont Drive. There were many docks along Edgemont Drive at that time, built by the homeowners for private use. (Katherine O'Grady.)

This is an early view of the home at 503 Edgemont. At the time this photograph was taken, c. 1919, the home was owned by Mr. and Mrs. J. Otto Rhome. With increased interest in this area as a summer resort, the Rhomes, like many other local residents, rented their homes during the summer months for considerable sums. (John O. Rhome Jr.)

John O. Rhome Jr. as a young boy with a scooter and wagon in front of the house at 503 Edgemont Drive. (John O. Rhome Jr.)

The Loch Arbour Hotel was built just after the turn of the century and soon became a popular alternative to the overcrowded hotels and rooming houses in Asbury Park. It was located along Edgemont Drive one block from the beach. The structure was torn down in the early 1960s and the property subdivided for residential use. (Robert Speck Collection.)

An aerial view of Edgemont Drive provides a visual image of this area at the time the photograph was taken in 1920. The several boat liveries on Deal Lake at this time, coupled with the proximity of the beach, made this a very attractive vacation location. (Dave Lumia.)

A 1917 postcard shows the Hotel Throckmorton just beyond the bridge which crossed Deal Lake from Grand Avenue (now Park Avenue) in Asbury Park to Main Avenue (now Norwood Avenue) in Loch Arbour. Of curious note are the utility poles which sprout throughout the lake. (Robert Speck Collection.)

The Hotel Throckmorton was located on the corner of Main and Edgemont Avenues. The structure was destroyed by fire in 1968. Today it is the site of several homes.

The Loch Arbour Baths and pavilions existed for many years on the site of the present public and private beach clubs .The beachfront in Loch Arbour was much more developed and resort oriented than it is today, whereas residential homes have taken the place of these earlier ocean front attractions. (Robert Speck Collection.)

The Belleview Apartments, located on Edgemont Drive, were created to serve the need of those wishing to spend their summer at the shore but not interested in purchasing or leasing one of the larger houses in the area. The apartments were destroyed by fire in the mid-1950s. (Robert Speck Collection.)

This postcard from the 1920s depicts the Asbury Park Fishing Club, which was located on Deal Lake at the inlet to the ocean adjacent to the Coast Guard station. Technically situated just over the border in Asbury Park, the fishing club added to Loch Arbour's attractions. The Belleview Apartments are visible just to the right. Following its demolition in the late 1920s, the Marine Grill, a very well-known restaurant, occupied this property (Robert Speck Collection.)

This is an ad which appeared in *The Shore Thing*, a weekly summer publication that was popular in the 1940s and 1950s with summer visitors. The original beach club offered its members wooden lockers and an indoor restaurant. (Alice Schultz.)

This happy group of bathers were photographed at the Loch Arbour beach on July Fourth weekend 1935. (Jane DeForest.)

124

A northeaster that hit the coast in early November of 1953 caused the collapse of the Village Beach Club at Loch Arbour. Several subsequent structures have also fallen to similar fates. (Lois and James Kiley.)

The existing Loch Arbour Beach Club was rebuilt following the destruction of a powerful northeaster in October 1993.

Hoffman's Stand and Boat Dock was located just over the Main Street Bridge along Deal Lake. The establishment rented canoes and row boats, pumped gas, and sold hot dogs, hamburgers, and ice cream—all from this modest little shack. In the mid-1950s a new structure was built on this site known as Harvey's. At that time the lake was filled in to the railroad tracks for use as a parking lot. (Selena Hoffman.)

SHORE DAIRIES

ALLENHURST   MANASQUAN
EXCLUSIVE
DISTRIBUTORS FOR THE FAMOUS MARLU FARM MILK

Shore Dairies operated this bottling plant in Loch Arbour on the corner of Main and Lake Avenue. It was one of the last dairies in the area to operate as a home-delivery service. The building was razed in the early 1950s and the Deal Lake Building now occupies a portion of the site. (Helen Pike.)

IN MEMORY OF
THE 240 GERMAN PASSENGERS
OF THE SHIP NEW ERA,
WRECKED OFF DEAL BEACH
NOV. 13TH, 1854.
ERECTED BY THE NEW ERA
MONUMENT ASSOCIATION OF N. J.
NOV. 13TH, 1892.
J. DEGENRING PRES. J. HELDT V.P.
H. SCHOENLEIN SEC. C. P. KUHL TREAS.
COMMITTEE.
C. MILLER H. G. BAUER
J. AUL C. F. SUPP.
C. BREMER

NEW ERA

On November 13, 1854, the vessel *New Era*, bound for New York from Bremerhaven, Germany, ran aground upon a sand bar off a portion of the coast known at that time as Deal Beach. Despite the noble attempts of wreckmaster Abner Allen and volunteers from the area, 240 passengers, most of German descent, perished. In November 1897, this monument in the Old First Methodist Church Cemetery in West Long Branch was erected to mark their final resting place.

Acknowledgments

An unanticipated benefit of working on a project of this nature is spending time and sharing information with many people who possess a deep appreciation of our past. With this is mind I wish to express my sincere thanks to the following kindhearted souls who shared information and photographs with me, for no particular reason except that I asked:

The Allenhurst Centennial Committee and Gerry Ann Greer Varley, Peter Avakian and Avakian Associates, Kevin Chambers, Hope Cleary, Lou Ellen Cohalan, George Cook Jr., Elizabeth Couse, the Deal Golf and Country Club, Jane Deforest, Marge and Paul Edelson, Joseph Eid, Lee Elmer, James Foley, Elizabeth Hardy, Karen and Walt Hazelrigg, Paul Imgrund, Lois and James Kiley, Peter Lucia, David Lumia, the Monmouth County Historical Association, George Moss Jr., Katherine O'Grady, the Ocean Township Historical Museum, Ruth Koerner Oliver, Kathy Parratt, Hunt Parry, John Rhody, John O. Rhome Jr., Theresa Ryan, Alice Schultz, Frederick A. Smith Jr., Ann Steen, David Stick, Bill Temme, Robert Todd, and Fred and Dorothy Wills. Special thanks for the assistance and encouragement of experienced Arcadia authors Randall Gabrielan, Helen-Chantal Pike, and Karen Schnitzpahn. Lastly, I would like to acknowledge Robert Speck, a lifelong Deal resident whose interest in history coupled with his generous nature was a contributing factor in the completion of this book.